TRAVELS
FOR A
DONKEY

TRAVELS
FOR A
DONKEY

Elisabeth D. Svendsen MBE

Whittet Books

This book is dedicated to Brian Bagwell, Deputy Administrator of the Sanctuary and my right hand. Without his skilful running of the Sanctuary in my frequent absences to help the donkeys abroad, none of this book's contents could have happened.

First published 1990
© 1990 by Elisabeth D. Svendsen

Whittet Books Ltd,
18 Anley Road, London W14 0BY

Design by Paul Saunders

The Donkey Sanctuary and the International Donkey Protection Trust are based at Sidmouth, Devon EX10 0NU

British Library Cataloguing in Publication Data
Svendsen, Elisabeth D.
Travels for a donkey.
1. Great Britain. Donkeys. Protection. Organisations.
International Donkey Protection Trust
I. Title
639.9′79725

ISBN 0–905483–78–2

Typeset by Phoenix Photosetting, Chatham, Kent
Printed and bound by South China Printing Co., Hong Kong

All photographs are by June Evers and Len Shepherd, with the exception of the following, which appear by kind permission of photographers: Daily Mail, p. 72, p. 74, p. 75(2), p. 76; Roy Harrington, p. 64; Elisabeth D. Svendsen, MBE, p. 17; Paul Svendsen, p. 22, p. 59.

PREVIOUS PAGE *An Ethiopian mule with a traditional harsh bit.*

OPPOSITE *Orphan's feeding time.*

Contents

1

Introduction

LOOKING through some old photographs the other day, I came across a faded photograph of a badly lamed white donkey being comforted by a vaguely familiar figure. A closer inspection (I need my glasses now) revealed a much younger version of myself; the place Tangiers, and the year 1958. Memory quickly returned of my horror, on my very first holiday from England, at the way donkeys were treated abroad. I am sure many animal lovers reading this book can recall holidays that were spoilt by the suffering animals they have witnessed, some suffering caused by ignorance, some by direct cruelty.

We feel, with some satisfaction, that donkeys in the UK have a very much higher quality of life than the millions working throughout the world, but it would be entirely wrong to take the view that all donkeys abroad are misused or ill-treated, and my travels for the donkey have led not only to tears, but also to happiness. I have had many adventures and experiences. My travels have, hopefully, led to a new awareness of the totally under-rated assistance millions of donkeys have given over thousands of years to help our species – man.

Having successfully set up the Donkey Sanctuary to cope with all the problems in the UK and also the Slade Centre, where donkeys, once rescued themselves, are able to help handicapped children, I turned my thoughts to the work abroad, and registered the International Donkey Protection Trust as a charity in 1976. From my holiday visits I knew the situation for donkeys abroad was bad, but since forming the International Donkey Protection Trust (IDPT) I have been frequently appalled at the conditions under which donkeys have to work and the way they are treated in many parts of the world.

According to recent figures published by the FAO there are 55 million donkeys in the world. From my own surveys I have doubts as to whether these figures are accurate, and they should really be used only as a guideline. To show why I am sceptical: we were told there were thousands of donkeys in a certain area of Turkey, and when we got there found one; 'tousands and tousands' of donkeys in a part of Ireland, where we saw five; we have discovered through experience that we could rarely rely on the printed statistics and we have learnt much and become wiser. The fact remains, however, that there are enormous problems for overseas donkeys and someone, somehow, has to tackle it.

PREVIOUS PAGE A donkey and his keeper in Lamu.

Demonstrating the damage overloading can do on an immature donkey.

2

Improving the Donkey's Working Conditions

THE work of the donkeys in the world varies depending on the terrain. This dictates whether their main use is as pack animals or draught animals or, more recently, tourist animals (see later chapter). Overloading on pack animals is a common problem, and very tempting to a poverty-stricken owner, often under-nourished himself and hoping the donkey can make the journey in one trip rather than two. Donkeys are so willing and biddable that they patiently accept crate after crate, stone after stone, shovel of sand after shovel of sand, until their legs actually buckle, and I am sad to say, I have actually seen them forced to their knees; only then, if the donkey is lucky, is the last 'straw' (in terms of load) removed; if unlucky, the donkey is the recipient of kicks and blows.

PREVIOUS PAGE *Water carrier in Mexico.*

BELOW *Overload of cereals in Ethiopia (note weight on donkey's legs).*

Loaded with coral in the traditional soggies.

Fortunately many donkeys are the lifeline of the family and as such are treated with a certain amount of respect. In Cyprus the donkeys live alongside the families, their main use being to help with the harvesting during the apple season, picking their way unerringly through the terraced orchards perched on the mountainside. At other times they fetch the wood for fuel, the water for drinking and the groceries from the village, which could be as far as ten miles away.

In Kenya the local people have designed a type of basket pannier, known as a 'soggie', which fits across the back of the donkey. This is an excellent method of carrying the maximum weight without causing sores to the donkey's back, but it can sometimes lead to overloading, as again there is a great temptation to add the extra concrete block, piece of coral or shovel of sand.

13

Arriving after a fifteen-mile walk to Debre Zeit market, Ethiopia.

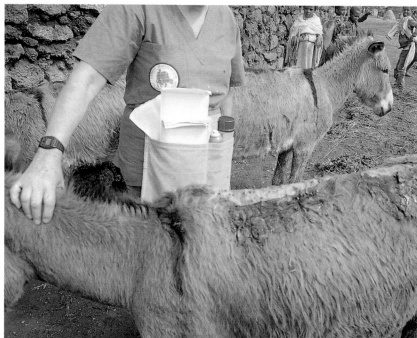

Fly infested back sore, Ethiopia.

In Ethiopia things are very much worse for the donkeys; no soggies or packs of any kind are available and the donkeys suffer the most distressing wounds on their backs caused by over-weighted sacks rubbing on the donkey's spine. In an attempt to help both countries we paid the Kenyan people on the island of Lamu the sum of £1 per soggie to make a thousand and these, not without great difficulty, we had shipped out to Ethiopia. Now some of the donkeys in the Debre Zeit area there are beginning to feel the benefit of this new system of loading. We are extremely hopeful that when other peasants realize how much more comfortably the donkey can carry an equal load they will be tempted to find materials available locally to make their own soggies or the equivalent.

All goods arriving in Lamu have to be carried by the donkey.

Perhaps one of the biggest loads we have seen carried was by a very tiny donkey, trudging with its enormous load of wood up a dual-carriageway in Ecuador. We stopped the car and ran back to catch a glimpse of this poor little donkey's face under the huge pile of wood. Despite the twigs being small they were in fact very heavy in bulk. We followed this donkey to its ultimate loading-place and were relieved to see the burden taken off and its obvious delight in being able to wander away and graze for a few moments before, no doubt, re-tracing its steps to bring yet another load.

Whilst on this trip in Ecuador we had an amusing experience. We had been left money in a legacy specifically to make a trip to Venezuela, Peru and Ecuador to survey the conditions for donkeys. I took Andrew Trawford, our vet at that time, June Evers, my colleague who has accompanied me on most of my trips, and Bob Forbes, a freelance reporter for BBC television who promised that with June photographing and him directing, the film taken could, hopefully, be shown on local television. Having photographed the poor little donkey trudging along with its terrible load, we pulled into a very small town for a lunch-time snack. It was a very spartan, bar-type restaurant and the self-service meal consisted of the most peculiar type of soup which had parts of some small animals' anatomy floating in it, alarmingly like the rodent species. However, in the middle of every table, to help down this rather tasteless food, was a bowl which contained an appetizing looking relish. In fact, it turned out to be one of the hottest chilli mixtures I think I've ever tasted. Bob Forbes, with his usual desire to taste new foods, took a spoonful and, dipping his finger on the spoon, took a mouthful, at which he spluttered and attempted to take a glass of water to stop the severe burning on his lips and fingers. Very quickly Andrew Trawford, who had worked in the area before, pushed the glass away and gave him the bowl of sugar, persuading him to dab it liberally on his lips and fingers. This immediately eased the pain, and apparently is the correct cure for chilli burns. We finished the rest of our meal and Bob retreated to the corner of the restaurant, where the 'senors' was to be found. I was just paying the bill at the counter while the others were sitting quietly talking, when the sounds of desperate yelling were heard from the 'senors'. Bob's bright red face appeared, obviously in agony, over the swing-type doors, as he shouted desperately 'sugar, sugar – quickly!'. Andrew Trawford had to rush into the facilities with, apparently, a very necessary bowl of sugar! That

Overloaded donkey in Ecuador.

evening, however, it was Bob's turn to laugh. We stayed in a remote motel, the rooms more like prison cells, each having a metal bunk-bed, and the communal 'facilities' at the end of the corridor consisted of one shower and one toilet. Andrew Trawford decided to have his shower and had just covered himself with soap and lather, when the water supply stopped completely – both hot and cold, and he was left covered in soapsuds in some embarrassment. We took it in turns to go with buckets to draw water from the outside well, which were passed to Andrew to throw over himself before he was able to appear in public again.

In many parts of the world the donkey is used as a draught animal, i.e. it pulls a cart or some sort of ploughing implement, generally alongside an ox or even a camel, as we have witnessed in the Middle East. A donkey's pulling power is much greater than its carrying power, provided of course that the harness fits and the cart to be pulled is balanced. Unfortunately these circumstances rarely occur and the usual thing is a far too heavy cart and tack that is more suitable for a horse or an ox, having been adapted with pieces of wire to fit the donkey. This not only results in uneconomical loads but causes great distress to the donkey. The Kikuyu tribe in Africa are particularly callous and I have frequently seen their donkeys collapsed at the side of the road, purely because the weight is taken on a band round the donkey's neck, and when straining up a hill this actually cuts off the air supply to the donkey. Education by the KSPCA (Kenya Society for the Protection and Care of Animals), situated in Nairobi, is gradually helping to prevent this terrible problem, but it is extremely difficult to change methods that have been in practice for many years.

OPPOSITE *Donkeys waiting for a return load in Kenya.*

Typical bad harnessing of donkey in Limuru, Kenya.

In Egypt one of the worst problems donkeys face when pulling carts is to find themselves owned by the Zebalines, who are the refuse men around Cairo. These poor donkeys, belonging to the refuse gatherers of Cairo, are harnessed to the most enormously heavy carts and are whipped and forced from the outskirts of Cairo up the steep cobbled hill to the refuse dump in the Mokattam Hills. These donkeys probably have one of the worst tasks in the world. The Brooke Hospital for Animals in Cairo visit with their mobile clinic, and we have helped provide them with money to ease the conditions. In fact we provided the funds for a water trough to be built for the Zebaline donkeys and have helped in as many ways as we can. For some years we worked alongside the Brooke Hospital in the markets, but it was jointly felt that perhaps the efforts of Europeans were resented more than those of the Egyptians and that it was better to leave them in charge of the situation. In 1987 we were, however, requested by the Veterinary Service of the Egyptian Ministry of Agriculture to start visiting again, not only to help with the bad conditions but to set up, with their co-operation, a worming programme. I am delighted to say that the ministry is now substantially helping where it is most needed.

On my recent visit to a market in Cairo a small girl stopped with her white donkey and cart at the first aid centre we had set up, and was highly delighted for her donkey, whom she obviously loved, to have medication put on its sores and a general check-up. We were accompanied by five vets from the university, who had advised us this was a donkey market; in fact it seemed on that particular day it was a camel market, and it was thought for some time we wouldn't find any work to do. However, I wandered away from the camels and found scores of suffering mules, donkeys and ponies carrying the many supplies being brought into the market. The small clinic worked flat-out, eventually with the aid of all the vets, who suddenly appreciated the enormous amount of work to be done.

Donkeys can be useful for ploughing, and in many countries they are used for this. Even if mechanical ploughs are given to impoverished farmers, the first mechanical breakdown can be an absolute catastrophe, as nobody has either the knowledge or the spare parts with which to carry out repairs, so there is no doubt donkeys are going to have to continue their work for many, many years to come. Again, problems suffered by donkeys have been caused by using the wrong equipment and, on a call to Gambia, we

Cairo market where donkeys are treated.

found to our horror that the donkeys (who were dying 'inexplicably') had not only been used with harness provided for oxen but also were expected to pull through the hard, dry, sandy earth metal or enormous wooden ploughs designed for oxen.

The first thing to do of course, under these conditions, is to ensure that the correct-sized equipment is used, and quite recently we were invited up to Shuttleworth Agricultural College where they are carrying out an excellent project for overseas students. Here the students are divided into groups, each group being given a different grade of implement, ranging from that which would only be found in the poorest of communities with no mechanical help whatsoever, to what might be provided by an up-to-date small engineering unit. Each group of students then had to produce a suitable piece of agricultural equipment to be pulled by either a donkey or an ox. We arrived in time to test out the results of

Donkey doing agricultural work in Mexico.

Mule demonstrating student's handmade plough at Shuttleworth Agricultural College.

Sanctuary donkeys in ploughing competition with John Rabjohns our manager in Devon.

the twelve-week course, and found it extremely interesting. The donkeys and mules were well able to cope with the equipment and I could see that these would be of immense value to the Third World. In addition, the fact that these trained students could now go back and spread their knowledge in their own countries would be of enormous help. We followed this up by purchasing one of the ploughs that they had designed and developed for the donkeys, and entered the local Colaton Raleigh Ploughing Association competition. Granted we were put in a separate class from the many beautiful tractors and highly trained agricultural workers driving them, but I am delighted to say that the donkeys got first prize in their class, whose contestants included two vintage tractors.

Returning to the problems in the Gambia on which we were asked to comment, we were distressed to find that not only were the donkeys expected to work with the wrong type of plough, but they had been brought from the Senegal area, and had not been inoculated against the tsetse fly. As you may well know, the bite of the tsetse fly develops into an awful disease called trypanosomiasis which is fatal to many equines and cattle. Even more upsetting was the callous attitude of the organizers who said, 'Well, there are plenty more cheap donkeys in the Senegal – it's not really a problem'. As you can imagine, we have done our best to change this point of view.

3

Preventive Medicine

ON studying the many uses that donkeys are put to in the Third World, it is easy to see their economic value; one of the tragedies of the past has been that these hard-working animals have been allowed to die at the age of 10 or 11 without any question as to the cause of death. Until we started our work and began to go round the world carrying a small laboratory to check the parasitic condition of donkeys, it was assumed that the natural lifespan of the donkey was only 11 years. At the Donkey Sanctuary the age expectancy of 1,600 donkeys is estimated at 37 years, and we have had donkeys of over 50 years. There was obviously some anomaly which could have been exacerbated by lack of food, lack of water and overwork, but, following my surveys, it became rapidly apparent that the biggest problem to donkeys in the Third World was parasites. Unfortunately the donkeys have a double problem; not only are they born to mares heavily infested themselves, but frequently they are unable to graze freely, being tethered in one area with a group of donkeys. The life cycle of the parasite that affects the donkeys dictates that the eggs are expelled to the ground; they hatch and the larvae then climb up the short grass stems and are re-ingested by the donkey. Donkeys not able to graze freely therefore continually re-ingest the larvae and keep the cycle going. Once their gut is completely full of parasites these parasites in fact begin to consume the food which the donkey itself should be using for nutrition and eventually begin to burrow out through the wall of the stomach. This causes small clots of blood, or embolisms, which are carried round the bloodstream to the heart and eventually kill the donkey.

One of the main ways that we can help donkeys throughout the world is by dosing them twice a year with an anthelmintic, a paste that kills parasites. This means that the donkey can take far more nourishment from the food it eats, which means it begins to get more flesh on its back and in turn means less sores for the donkey. So one of our biggest jobs to help donkeys in the Third World is to persuade governments to co-operate with us in setting up worming programmes to get rid of the parasites. I must now have travelled around almost every Third World country where donkeys are used, and the results are most encouraging.

Quite obviously our preventive treatment is the best way in which we can assist the donkey; it means liaising with veterinary universities and agricultural officers throughout the world, and this the IDPT has done. Although we have limited funds, we have

*Lamu owner feeds
orphaned foal in Lamu
Sanctuary.*

been able to provide anthelmintics and set up small trials; we have been able to prove, not only to the owners of the donkeys, but to the government veterinary surgeons working with us, the tremendous advantage in the stature and well-being of the donkey once we have rid it of parasites.

When we first visited Lamu, a small island off the east coast of Kenya, it was a common sight to see the drover pulling hard on his rope, dragging a team of donkeys with very heavy loads. Now it is far more common to see a group of donkeys walking briskly under their loads, with the drover having to hold them back. The donkeys obviously must feel much fitter and more able to cope with their day's work.

On my first visit to Lamu, with great difficulty, I managed to persuade local people to bring their donkeys along to have a dose of anthelmintic. Abdalla Hadi Rifai, who later became our manager, was our interpreter, and tried to explain the reason for giving

Animal friendship in Lamu.

Bahati's foal in Matondoni (see p. 41).

Clinic in Matondoni, Kenya.

the donkeys the dose of worming paste, which is inserted by a small syringe into the donkey's mouth. The fact that the donkeys might have worms in the stomach had obviously never occurred to the locals, and I think they thought we were more than a little crazy to insist on dosing all the donkeys. We were, however, able to dose some thirty to forty animals, and had to be satisfied with this number. The following morning, as I was walking up the road, I was surprised to hear a commotion from behind. Turning round, I saw a man running up to me holding a small piece of newspaper, in which something was carefully nestling, shouting, 'Dudus, dudus!' Everybody gathered round as he met me. He pushed the newspaper under my nose for me to see the contents, and there sat

'Dudus' in Lamu.

A close look at the 'dudus', with the worms clearly visible.

a large pat of donkey dung, from out of which thousands of worms were wriggling. 'Dudus, dudus!' (the Swahili name for worms is 'dudu') he shouted again, pushing the offending item under the noses of all those standing around, and obviously explaining that our medicine had actually worked. This practical demonstration was of the most immense value to us; nothing I said would have acted so well as that one man running up the street, and I think the fortunes of the donkeys in Lamu must have changed from that moment.

It is now a fact that, whereas in the past we dosed the donkeys with no problem at all, the donkeys standing quietly and docilely while we gave them the paste through the mouth, and treated any sores, they are now becoming quite difficult to treat. They are obviously feeling fully fit and able to physically object quite strongly to our ministrations.

Every time we carry out a dosing session we also hold a clinic, and of course education is a very large part of our work. As I have mentioned previously, very few people who depend on donkeys for their livelihood are deliberately cruel to them; cruelty is mainly due to ignorance and lack of understanding of the donkey's needs. On the island of Lamu we have set up a small sanctuary and are

A typical street scene in Lamu showing that donkeys are the only mode of transport possible.

there to stay; Lamu is a very old town with extremely narrow streets, and every item of building material or food has to arrive by sea. There is no way any mechanical vehicle can wend its way through the narrow streets, so donkeys are the only mode of transport. The sanctuary not only makes sure every animal on Lamu, and the surrounding islands (3,800 of them), is dosed for parasites but also takes in donkeys who have been attacked by hyenas or have succumbed to trypanosomiasis or tetanus. The sanctuary administers treatment to those donkeys in need and when fit again they are returned to their owners.

To help encourage the locals to look after their donkeys properly we hold an annual competition. The prizes given are very substantial, so that it is in everybody's interest to make sure their donkey is looked after throughout the year and brought to the competition in peak condition. There is great excitement on competition day, which is generally on December 12th, one of Kenya's national holidays. This year, the fourth year of the contest, we held a separate competition for the best kept foal. We were able to demonstrate to the children, who are frequently the donkey minders, the damage they can do by over-loading the donkeys at too young an age. By pressing a hand lightly on the foal's back we clearly showed them the weakness of the spine. Donkeys should not carry any loads until at least three years of age. Having held these competitions, the local people are now well aware of what is required and what the best donkeys look like. It is one of the most interesting days of the year when 'Donkey Competition Day' comes round in Lamu.

Winners of the competition in Lamu, 1988.

Hopeful contestants in Lamu.

Because the donkeys in Lamu, when approached by humans, are usually being asked to work, they don't seem quite as friendly as those in the UK. However, I was highly delighted to find that the donkeys taken into care in the Lamu sanctuary, which have a chance to get used to humans as friends and companions, had changed completely; their normal beautiful nature had emerged. I was amused to see one of our little donkeys lying fast asleep on his back, his legs neatly tucked onto his chest, more like a sea otter than a donkey, and I couldn't resist going up to have a word with him. I was convinced he would jump up and run away, but to my surprise he just lay there, with the sun on his stomach, and thoroughly enjoyed being stroked – all at peace with the world.

Working on the other islands around Lamu is also tremendously interesting. Once again donkeys are the only mode of

Lying fast asleep, legs neatly tucked on his chest.

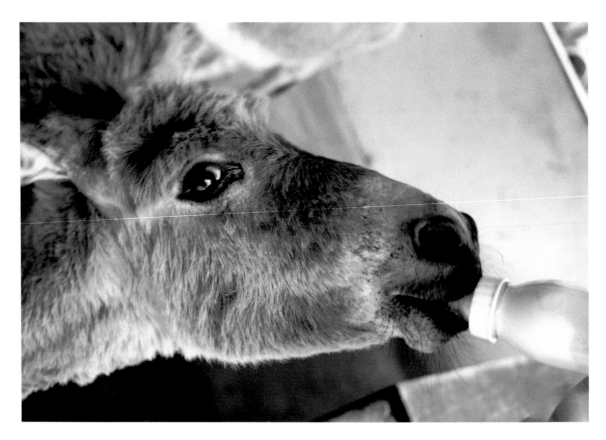

Enjoying a bottle.

transport on these isolated small Indian Ocean islands, and the only way to get to them is by boat. Our team visits regularly to dose the donkeys for parasites and is accompanied by a local veterinary officer. A great deal of stamina is needed to cope not only with the heat, which is frequently over 100° Fahrenheit, but with the long walks across islands to villages totally inaccessible except by foot. Sometimes the team has to walk up to twelve miles, carrying all its equipment, in addition to holding exhausting clinics at each location. However, the thanks of the local people and the improvement in the donkeys' well-being over the years has proved how well worthwhile the effort is.

On the island of Lamu, apart from the main town, there are two villages, one of which is called Matondoni. Once again this must be reached by boat and our team has been making regular visits to Matondoni over the years. On a visit in March 1987 we were appalled to find one of the most emaciated and sick-looking donkeys we had seen on our trips. This emaciated donkey was about eight years old and was brought to us by an obviously

Bahati on arrival at the Sanctuary.

heartbroken, caring owner, who was extremely elderly. A medical examination of the donkey showed that she was not only riddled with parasites but had been affected by trypanosomiasis and it seemed almost impossible that she could survive. The donkey's name was Bahati and the owner was almost in tears as we explained that her chance of survival was very slim. He asked if there was any way we could help. We told him that if he could take the donkey to Lamu town, where we had purchased premises, although workmen were still there, we would take Bahati in and see what we could do for her. We imagined that he would bring her by boat, and were very surprised two days later to find the old man walking into the sanctuary premises alongside a completely exhausted Bahati. Although Bahati's chances seemed extremely poor, we immediately set to work and she was given the necessary injections, vitamin supplements and much needed food. We had to be very careful worming her, as too large a dose in her weakened state could possibly have killed her, so this was done with the greatest possible care.

The Lamu Sanctuary.

Transport to the islands.

Three months later we returned to Lamu for the official opening of the sanctuary which took place on July 4th, perhaps to be known as Independence Day for the donkeys in Lamu. I was absolutely delighted to find the immense change in Bahati. She had already put on weight, and instead of looking so desperately sick and having completely lost interest in life, she was much brisker and quite obviously well on the road to recovery. I had the great pleasure of inviting her owner to the opening ceremony and then had the joy of seeing him and Bahati set off on their walk home. The old man said goodbye and kissed me with tears in his eyes. It was a very moving experience.

Just thirteen months later, on our regular visit to Matondoni, we were surprised to see practically the whole village waiting for us as our boat anchored in the soft mud as near to the village as we

Bahati going home with her owner.

were able to get. Struggling with all our equipment through the thick mud, I was surprised to see one of the people in the crowd rush forward, stumbling through the mud, regardless of his long robes which dragged behind him, and alarmed to find that he fell on his knees at my feet, calling, 'Bahati – m'toto, m'toto.' He had tears pouring down his face and I realized that it was Bahati's owner. For a heart-stopping moment I was sure Bahati had died, and turned to Abdalla, our manager and interpreter, and asked, 'Abdalla, what's happened, has Bahati died?' Abdalla grinned cheerfully and pointed up to the crowd of villagers standing with a

Bahati and foal on Lamu island.

rather plump-looking donkey and next to her, the sweetest little foal I had ever seen. This was Bahati's 'm'toto', the African name for a baby foal. To everybody's joy and surprise, Bahati had recovered magnificently, enough to present her poor owner with the gift of a little foal. The welcome we received that day in Matondoni was out of this world. Coconut matting had been laid for us to work on and instead of the usual eight donkeys arriving for treatment, over a hundred appeared, the leader of the village having been so impressed with Bahati's progress that he had insisted that every person brought their donkey to be dosed. The villagers had even gone to the extent of getting Coca Cola for us to drink; an absolute luxury, and very greatly appreciated.

In my constant efforts to alert vets throughout the world to the donkey's needs, and to point out the basic differences in the physiology of the donkey to that of the horse, I have put together a *Professional Handbook*, with vital information collated from veterinarians with experience of surgery, anaesthesia and clinical treatment of the donkey.

I have also had the privilege of giving papers at the Conferences of the World Association for the Advancement of Veterinary Parasitology, where vets drawn from throughout the world gather to hear and discuss the latest developments in the fight for animal health. It is always a nerve-racking experience. I am usually the only unqualified person to give a paper, and at my first meeting, in Rio de Janeiro, my paper was on the last day; for some reason, having been scheduled in one of the smaller rooms which only seated about sixty people and had a nice informal atmosphere, my talk was moved to the main hall, with instant interpretation into three languages and an enormous audience. I was quite terrified, but fortunately, as mine was probably less scientific and a change from the mass of technical details everyone had been absorbing, they found my practical talk a change and the response to my plea for help for millions of donkeys met with a most sympathetic and enthusiastic reception. They must have enjoyed it, because one American association invited me to Atlanta to speak at their congress. This year's meeting is in East Berlin, and we are inviting five of the vets working for us overseas to give papers on the progress we are making, and to up-date the situation for all concerned. I expect my knees will be knocking again.

One of the other areas in which we spend a lot of time is Mexico. There are over six million donkeys in Mexico and again they play a very important part in the economy of the country.

In the years that we have worked there, we have begun to see a gradual improvement, not only in the physical appearance of the donkeys, but in the way they are regarded by their owners. Capula was one of the small villages chosen for our anthelmintic trial, lying some 120 miles south-east of Mexico City. We worked closely with Dr Aline de Aluja from the Mexican Veterinary University and two of her graduates, Enrique Nunez and Guillermo Rodriguez. We would arrive at the village at around 8.30 a.m. to find hardly a soul in sight – the dusty village tracks deserted, apart from the odd old man slumped, suffering from the effects of last night's tequila, and

The dusty street in Capula, Mexico.

the inevitable small dirty children grouped together by the squalid houses. Driving up the track we would arrive at an equally deserted sports field – a square of sand surrounded by high cacti. After stopping the vehicle and beginning to unload our medical gear, the church bell would begin to toll at the other end of the village, as a signal we had arrived, and, as if by magic, small strings of donkeys appeared from all directions to converge on our group. Within thirty minutes we would be hard at work, in the midst of a crowd.

Because the peasants were so poor, a small amount had to be paid to each one to compensate them for losing their donkey's labour for half an hour. At first everything ran smoothly; all were paid equally and were happy; but gradually we ran into trouble. To

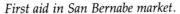

First aid in San Bernabe market.

The wood barter market in Mexico.

prove to the government and the peasants that the treatment really worked, we selected, thoroughly examined and graded sixty donkeys. The donkeys were then identified by a photograph, age and medical condition, and documented with a number and the owner's name. Twenty of the donkeys were given Eqvalan, twenty given an alternative wormer and twenty given a 'placebo' (a paste with no medication at all). For the first two visits, all went well, but by the third, those whose donkeys were receiving the placebo dose were not so happy. The donkeys on Eqvalan were suddenly much fitter and stronger, and looked fatter. The donkeys on the alternative wormer worked better too, but those receiving the placebo had remained the same, and that did not please their owners, who felt their donkeys were worse than those of their friends.

Again and again all over the world those donkeys dosed have improved out of all recognition, and great care has been taken to look after the placebo animals at the end of each trial.

Sores, sorrow and malnutrition in San Bernabe market.

An almost impossible task in Debre Zeit market.

One of our big problems in Ethiopia also has been selecting animals for the trials, and three different villages were selected here. Once again the results were quite amazing. On my last visit, the first area we went to was the placebo area, and we met with a very off-hand reception. They did bring their donkeys in and in this case we had provided the Faculty of Veterinary Medicine at Addis Ababa University with a collar for every donkey with its identification number on, and it was very difficult to see any difference in the donkeys in this area at all – all were miserable, had no energy and were in need of a great deal of help. As this was the last trip of the year's trial we were able to take dung samples from these donkeys to check the parasitic infestation, and then give them their first proper dose of anthelmintic, which we knew would start to improve their general condition. In the next village

All were miserable and had no energy.

Explaining to the villagers the need for anthelmintics.

we went to we found a different story. Here they had been given one of the other anthelmintics we had used, which was not so good as Eqvalan but had still made an impressive difference on the animals in the trial. The villagers were much happier to stay and talk to us, and to make sure all the donkeys in the trial were rounded up for the final administration and for the collection of the dung samples. The head of the village, called Ato Yeshaw Kassay, came and told me how very important the donkey was to the working peasants in Ethiopia; in fact he categorically stated that in his opinion the donkey was the key to the economic survival of the poor farmers and people in Ethiopia. These village heads are extremely important in their countries, and as most of Ethiopia now works on a communal basis, he directs where the efforts of the village should be placed on a daily basis, and controls the agricultural plan for his area.

In the third village the donkeys were in excellent condition.

Having left the village, followed by the usual dogs and waving people, we then progressed to the third and final village which lay about four miles away over very rough roads. Here the sight that met our eyes was fantastic. As we drove past the squalid huts in which the half-clothed children and adults huddled, and arrived in the countryside, we were suddenly surrounded by a glorious group of galloping donkeys. The donkeys kept pace with our vehicle until we came to the village; each one had a red collar round its neck, and was in what can only be described as 'excellent condition'. The whole village came out to meet us, laughing and shouting, and their delight at the different appearance of the donkeys, and the donkeys' ability to happily and strongly help them now in their efforts was very apparent.

We try to help these people, not only in a practical way, but through education, and I was delighted that same evening to be asked to give a lecture at the Veterinary University to a group of approximately sixty agricultural experts, veterinary officers and officials who were attending a meeting in an attempt to resolve the economic problems being met in Ethiopia. After my talk, in which I outlined the enormous value of the donkey and how the

Work in the markets is unending.

government could help us in extending the donkey's working life by making it fitter to help the community, it was question-time. One of the visiting agricultural officers stood up and said that he would just like to say that I had now solved a problem which had been worrying him for some time. Apparently one of the world organizations had made an offer to the Agricultural Department. This offer was for a gift to fifty villages selected in Ethiopia of either an ox, a donkey or ten goats; the choice to be theirs. He said he had been absolutely amazed that every single village had chosen the donkey, but having heard my talk on the unlimited uses the donkey was put to in his country, he could now understand their reasoning. Unfortunately the really poorest people in Ethiopia, those who I have seen sitting hopelessly in the markets surrounded by children with their only item for sale perhaps four flattened and dried pats of donkey dung, which are used as fuel, cannot even afford a donkey. We have now arranged with the Faculty of Veterinary Medicine in Debre Zeit that thirty of the donkeys to be used in the final trial will then be kept by our charity and loaned out free of charge on a daily basis to the poorest of the community, to enable them to carry water and food to their homes.

Great interest is shown in the work but conditions are not always easy.

These specially cared-for donkeys, in the peak of condition, will have to be returned each evening, when they will be fed and watered. At least a few people in the area should be helped by this, and by fitting the donkeys with proper soggies and showing how they should be kept, a good example will be given to both government authorities and people alike. This project is just starting and we are very hopeful that it will make a real contribution to this part of the world.

Working conditions in Ethiopia for the visiting team are in fact the worst we have anywhere in the world. One of the greatest problems is water for drinking; obviously untreated water can cause problems for our team, and on our last visit we were horrified to find that the bottling plant had closed down and it was impossible to obtain any type of mineral water. The water supply at the hotel is also very restricted and sometimes we return from markets where we have been not only treating donkeys with horrific and suppurating sores, but also doing our best to give first aid to humans who may be suffering from anything from leprosy to elephantiasis down to scabies, and frequently we would give everything we have for the joy of even cold water – hot water and baths being a luxury never afforded to us in this part of the world. The situation for people working there now has become so bad that in fact myself and my lifelong friend, June Evers (we met on our first day at school at five years old), are the only two from the International Donkey Protection Trust who will visit to work in this particular area.

It became obvious that a great deal of time needed to be spent in Mexico, not only on anthelmintics but on general donkey welfare, including foot care. So a mobile clinic has been set up, operating from Mexico City and manned by a full-time vet employed by the IDPT. One interesting market we visited was a wood barter market – no money changed hands, all goods were purchased by wood. Many of the goods sold and the wood itself

The first trip of the mobile clinic in Mexico.

Clinic in Ethiopia.

were brought in by donkeys. On our second visit we parked the medical van on the street, next to a poor donkey tied to a telegraph pole with terribly long cracked hooves. After three hours working with the donkeys and with Guillermo, our vet, explaining donkeys' needs to the people, we returned to find the donkey still there. Guillermo got out his farriery equipment, and in ten minutes an immaculately trimmed little donkey stood a lot more comfortably, waiting for his owner. A nasty sore had been treated on his hoof with our purple teramycin spray, so he did look slightly colourful. As we sat in the van ready to drive off, an extremely drunken Mexican weaved his way up the street – he stopped and looked at the donkey and was about to undo the rope, when his eyes fixed on the donkey's purple legs and trim hoofs. Leaving the rope and the donkey, he set off up the street with an extremely puzzled expression. He obviously thought he had the wrong animal. Guillermo climbed down from the van, and courteously followed him, bringing him back, explaining what he had done. Our last sight on leaving the village was the donkey setting off with the villager half asleep on his back, obviously knowing every step of the way home, but for once they were going to be comfortable steps.

The donkey with bad feet before being treated.

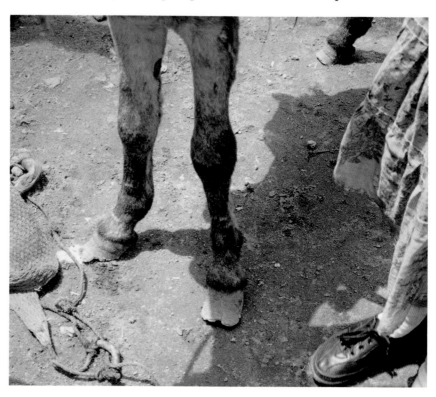

A heavy weight for a tiny donkey in Mexico.

Typical Mexican scene.

San Bernabe market, however, is another story, probably the worst market we visit in the world, where the overcrowding and loading of donkeys, ponies and horses into trucks is inhumane, and conditions for these animals, often on their way to the slaughterhouse, are intolerable. Much has to be done here, but I won't report fully, as I don't feel it's the best subject for a photographic book.

Animals arriving in San Bernabe market.

RIGHT *Intolerable loading conditions for horses and donkeys.*

4

Defending the Donkey Against Exploitation

WE also help donkeys used for the tourist trade. My first experience of this was in Santorini, Greece, where the donkeys are forced up the 597 steps of the cliff, carrying passengers and luggage from the boats and cruise ships. It was while investigating this in 1976 that I had a terrible accident when I fell down the hold of the yacht, breaking five ribs and puncturing my liver. I spent a very uncomfortable four weeks in a Greek hospital. Now, thanks to pressure by the IDPT and with help from the Greek Government, a telpherage has been installed to save the donkeys having to carry the heavy tourists up the hill, but unfortunately many of the tour operators, although mentioning the telepherage, add a rider in their brochures saying, 'However, it's much more fun on the donkeys.'

Donkeys also work hard for tourists in Mijas, Spain. A

PREVIOUS PAGE *The donkey coming out of the Town Hall at Villanueva de la Vera.*

BELOW *Donkey transport in Mijas.*

donkey taxi service operates regularly, and we have received complaints regarding this for very many years. However, we now have the services of a retired veterinary surgeon who lives in Spain. He visits Mijas every two weeks during the summer and once a month in the winter to check the donkeys' condition, their equipment, and to ensure they are able to do the work they are being asked to do.

We also have problems with donkey safaris. Many tourists regard this as the highlight of their holiday and happily go off on coaches to find a miserable group of skinny donkeys waiting to take them perhaps one and a half miles to a grubby tent which has been erected where dubious drinks and the never-ending supply of souvenirs are offered. The majority of times no attempt whatsoever is made to match rider with donkey and it is quite common to see an eighteen-stone man riding a tiny donkey of no more than nine hands. The IDPT has drawn up a Code of Practice with the co-operation of the Spanish Government, who have been very helpful, and hopefully this will soon become law throughout the whole of Spain.

Whilst on the subject of Spain, one cannot of course, leave this area without referring to the other side of the donkey work abroad, which is following up complaints of cruelty, and standing up for donkeys being abused in any way. I think most people are aware of the problems in Villanueva de la Vera following the enormous press publicity two years ago. On that occasion a donkey called Blackie was chosen to be dragged through the village during its religious ceremony, ridden by the fattest man in the village. A thick rope was put round Blackie's neck and approximately fifty knots made in the rope. Each of the men of the village was allocated a knot, and with fifty dragging the terrified Blackie the 'parade' began. On this occasion the fate that befell the donkey the previous year, when the donkey fell and was crushed to death by the crowd, was avoided, and eventually, helped by the press, in particular the *Star*, Blackie was purchased and eventually we were able to bring him back safely to our Donkey Sanctuary in Devon, where today he is fit, well and nothing like the terrified animal that we brought home. Last year the victim was a donkey nicknamed Beauty Thatcher but because of the enormous press outburst the previous year and because of the representations we had made to the Mayor and his assurance to us that the donkey would not be harmed, a ring of men linked arms and protected Beauty Thatcher as she was led through the streets. Even so, the firing of twelve-bore guns around her ears, the drums, the shouting and the enormous crowds, caused great distress to the donkey, who was literally shaking when we got to her at the end of her ordeal.

I don't think there is any way that we are going to be able to change the ways of the Spanish over their festivals and fiestas, but the public was absolutely fantastic in helping us in our efforts. We sent letters to King Juan Carlos, to the Ministry of Agriculture, to the Spanish Ambassador, and to the Mayor of the village, and petitions from all those involved in animal welfare. A grand total of 25,300 letters were sent, and these were obviously one of the main reasons that Beauty Thatcher was so well protected. I had been worried ever since the event as to how we could possibly alleviate the terror and suffering of the donkey used in this festival, and eventually came up with the idea that if we could make a suitable mock donkey, stable and strong enough to carry the heaviest man in the village and able to endure the dragging and abuse that the real donkey met with, perhaps we could persuade the village people to accept this donkey.

Every year Donkey Week is held at the sanctuary and people come from all over the world to spend a week with us in Sidmouth, enjoying themselves with the donkeys and making friends, and last year we decided to invite the Mayor of Villanueva de la Vera and his wife to come to our Donkey Week to attend the big luncheon held on the Sunday and, of course, to meet Blackie. We also intended to introduce to them the idea of the model donkey that they would hopefully use at the next year's festival. All seemed to be going very well until the actual day, when we learnt that the Mayor himself could not come, but he had sent his Minister for Tourism. She turned out to be a very nice lady, but when put in a field with Blackie to satisfy the 'gentlemen of the press', she proved to be absolutely terrified of donkeys and the resulting pictures turned out quite amusing. She promised she would go back and try her best to persuade the village to accept the model we were about to have made.

You can imagine the enormous disappointment when our offer of help was refused, as the village preferred to use a real donkey. However, nothing ventured, nothing gained, and we went ahead and produced a Blackie II. We introduced Blackie to Blackie II shortly before leaving for Villanueva de la Vera in February 1989, and, as you can see, he was quite surprised, but very

Blackie and Lola with the Minister for Tourism from Villanueva de la Vera.

Blackie II – the model donkey.

impressed, to see his double. In due course Blackie II was loaded onto the horse box and Neil Harvey and June Evers set off with the task of getting through the customs and meeting me in Madrid at the airport. A photographer and a reporter from the *Daily Mail* accompanied me and I took the precaution of taking an interpreter, Trini Hanson, who is Spanish but has lived in England for the last fifteen years. We should have been warned by the welcome we got at Madrid airport. To bring the car and horse box into the airport car park June and Neil had deposited the necessary money into the ticket machine, the barrier had lifted, but unfortunately, as the car went through, the barrier dropped before the horse box had time to clear, and this resulted in our first difficult meeting with the Spanish people. They did however take it in reasonably good part, and if only the rest of the trip had been the same I would have been very much happier.

We arrived safely in Jarandilla de la Vera at the Parador Hotel, some miles from the village of Villanueva de la Vera. Despite frantic telephone calls, we were unable to make contact with anybody in the village; we desperately wanted to do this, so that we could introduce Blackie II to them before the three-day drinking bout really got under way. Having no more luck the following morning, Trini left a message with the Town Hall to say that we were coming in and would be there at 11 o'clock. We set off with the horse box complete with Blackie II, and in the car following were Bob and Jim from the *Daily Mail*. We parked the car on the outskirts of the village where the ceremony takes place, and, leaving Neil with the horse box, walked down to the Town Hall. Unfortunately neither the Mayor nor the Minister for Tourism were there, but, very kindly, the gentleman in charge agreed he would try to find them. We made our way to one of the small cafés in the square to wait. Even at this stage we were subject to a certain amount of hassle from people who realized who we were and kept shouting, 'Burro, burro,' at us in a rather menacing manner. After an hour, the Minister for Tourism, Eugenia Miguel Fraile arrived, but the smile was quickly wiped off her face when we explained we had actually brought the false donkey with us. She said, 'There will be terrible trouble, because the villagers don't want it.' I was then worried about Neil, the driver, waiting with the vehicle at the top of the village. June Evers, my colleague, went to check he was all right and rapidly returned saying, 'There's quite an aggressive gang round him, and they're chanting slogans.' We quickly returned. The gang had managed to climb up on the box to look in and were vitriolic that we should be suggesting that anything other than a live donkey be used for their festival. A very heated discussion took place with much shouting and threatening, before we decided it was safer to move the horse box out of the area for a short time, until we were able to contact the Mayor. It was lucky we decided this, as a gang armed with axes were approaching when we drove off.

Eventually we managed to get the Mayor out of his office and we took him to meet Blackie II. The Mayor was extremely impressed with the size and strength of the donkey and the special precautions we had made to ensure the specially fitted castors would run over their thickly cobbled streets. However, he shook his head in dismay at the reception he thought the villagers would give to it. He explained to us that the attitude of the villagers was split and he was very much afraid that there would be bloodshed if the donkey was brought into the village. However, he cheered us up slightly by telling us he would put it to a meeting that afternoon at 5 o'clock. He thought probably if we just said it was a present for the village, we would be able to leave it in the main square, and although they wouldn't use it this year, maybe they would use it the next. The Mayor arranged to meet us that evening in the next village, and he, his wife and the Minister for Tourism would dine with us at 8.30.

Imagine our disappointment when nobody turned up and we received a very curt message to say they couldn't be with us and no news of how the village had reacted to our suggestion. We decided to keep very quiet on the Sunday, but on the Monday, when we had still heard nothing, we knew something had to be done. Neil Harvey and Trini slipped into the village with two jobs in mind; the first was to try and bribe the villagers so that our photographers could use a balcony to try and film the fiesta, safely out of the way of the mob, and secondly to try and find Eugenia so that we could establish what had happened at the meeting. Back at the hotel, we had a very tense time waiting for them, nor was it easy for Neil and Trini in the village, although fortunately they were not recognized. It appeared that there was no chance Blackie II could be taken in. They had managed to arrange a balcony for us, but the general feeling was that it would be unsafe for any of us to come into the village on the Tuesday – the day the poor donkey was actually to be used.

The *Daily Mail* men were so disappointed they weren't going to get any photographs of Blackie II with the villagers, they asked us if we would be prepared to take him to the next village to see their reaction. So off we departed into the mountains with the mock donkey. To our joy a fiesta was just finishing in a village about five miles away. When we opened the back of the horse box and took out the donkey, the locals went mad, and thoroughly enjoyed it. We ran the donkey up and down the street with people riding it, dancing and singing, and we all thought what a contrast to Villanueva, and how lovely it would be if they would only do this.

The following morning, very tense, we arrived in the village just before 9 o'clock. The ceremony was due to start at 10.15 a.m. and immediately we were met with the most hostile reception I think I've ever had. We were threatened with being put in the fountain in the village square, being beaten with ropes and sticks, and even twelve-bore shotguns were waved in our direction, but at this stage not fired. Graffiti, which was not complimentary to the English, had been written all over the walls of the Town Hall, and there was no mistaking the menacing attitude of the drunken mob who were to handle the poor donkey selected. My heart sank, as did those of the team. We had now been joined by our vet, Derek Baker, who works for us in Spain, and he too felt extremely concerned at the obvious anger of the crowd. We got the photographers up on the balcony as safely as we could, but within half an hour of the event starting they too were having guns pointed at them, and by this time people were actually beginning to fire the twelve-bores, which, although purportedly emptied by them and filled with toilet paper, seemed to contain something that was causing damage to many of the balconies and to anything they fired at.

At the appointed time the Town Hall doors opened and about nine men pulling the long rope with the fifty knots on, hurled out into the square, shouting, firing guns and yelling, which marks the start of the ceremony. We knew that at some stage the donkey was going to be attached to the rope and pulled out, but there are many false starts, and you never know when it will be, and in fact on this occasion, fifteen times they burst out of the Town Hall, at one time trying to get the rope round us, which would have caused a fair amount of distress and injury. On the sixteenth time, out came the donkey, to our horror already forced to his knees and terrified from

RIGHT *Blackie II was welcomed to the festival in the next village.*

Gunman reloading shotgun.

the guns that had been fired inside the Town Hall. We set off to follow the donkey round its terrible trail through the village, dragged by the drunken, shouting, jeering, firing mob, and at this stage June Evers determinedly came off the balcony to join in and to help protect me, as I had become the main target for their hate. It was a good job she did come. We were frequently fired at – and at one point a gun blasted a plant pot over my head, which showered us all. At another point a wedge of three men ran into us at full speed, knocking me flat to the ground, and hurling June and Neil into the walls of the houses of the narrow street through which we were passing.

If it was bad for us, it was horrendous for the donkey. Four times he fell completely and our hearts were bleeding for this poor animal, as he was subjected to the pushes, kicks and sticks waved in his direction, not to mention fireworks under his feet and guns around his ears. At the end of one hour and seventeen minutes we returned to the town square amongst the terrifying mob. Usually, at this stage the donkey is allowed to come to us. However, this time it took a further seven minutes before he was strong enough to stand and stagger in our direction. We then managed to get him away from the mob and eventually back to his stable, but it was a most terrifying experience and one which we feel should never be allowed to happen again.

We received enormous support from everybody, and have written to all we can think of who could help: the Pope, King Juan Carlos, the Spanish Ambassador, our Royal Family and Members of the European Parliament. Owing to an epidemic of African horse sickness in Spain this year, there was never any chance we could have brought the donkey back; no equines can be moved for a period of at least six months, and so the poor donkey has had to stay in Spain, although the village will have no further interest in him now his part has been played and the press has gone. We are rather hopeful that the Italian and Spanish television crews, both of whom received rough treatment at the hands of the crowd, and were in fact forced to retire halfway through the ceremony, will have shown their films in their respective countries and possibly aroused the wrath of other animal lovers throughout the world.

OVERLEAF: LEFT, TOP *The threatening crowd.* LEFT *The donkey at the end of its ordeal.* RIGHT *The donkey being dragged through the streets by its head.* RIGHT BELOW *At long last I got the donkey and could lead it away.*

73

With the Spanish Ambassador; trying to get a point across.

At the time of writing this book, February 1989, the reception of the Spanish Embassy in London has been excellent; they seem determined to help us in preventing a live donkey being used in future and have agreed to accept the mock donkey, which they will see is presented to the village by officials from Madrid. We all feel it may be more acceptable coming from their own people than from outsiders.

5 The Poitou

SOME breeds of the donkey are now in danger of dying out: the Onager, the Somali Wild Ass and the Poitou, for instance. We are at the moment trying to help the French to protect the endangered Poitou donkey, probably one of the most unusual and beautiful breeds in the world. Bred in the Poitou area of France, they were once mated with a particular breed of horse, the mulassier, to produce one of the strongest mules in the world. This mule, bred since the Middle Ages, was used in two world wars and was extremely strong and sturdy. Now lack of demand has led to a drop in the population to around sixty at the maximum. Inbreeding has caused many problems, but through a joint effort by the French

With Jonquille (a Poitou donkey).

and ourselves, we hope to reverse the trend and prevent these large, beautiful creatures from becoming extinct.

The world is full of animals, large and small, beautiful and ugly, intelligent and stupid; there is a place for them all, but there is one that I feel has been for too long totally ignored and underrated – the gentle donkey, who has worked harder for man than any other species and who, up until recently, could expect no reward. Let us hope our humble work will be taken up by all to make this world a better place for both man and donkey.

Millions of donkeys need our help.